ABORTION FACTS

Conrad Birmingham

INTRODUCTION

I am shocked at the number of people amazed at the number of deaths over the past fifty years from abortions. The number is more than sixty million. Yes, sixty million babies have been killed since Roe v Wade. They call me a liar when I tell them billions of babies have been killed worldwide since 1980 from abortions. This is the reason for this book, so people know the facts. This book is a simple archive of abortion facts—actual numbers from sources accounting for the number of abortions in the United States and worldwide.

I hope you are aware of the numbers, and if you are not, this will give you an idea of the mass murder taking place in the United States and in the world.

CONTENTS

Centers for Disease Control and Prevention

Centers for Disease Control and Prevention

World Health Organization

https://www.who.int/news-room/fact-sheets/detail/abortion

Other Deaths in Comparison to Abortion

Abortion Facts

U.S. Abortions – 60 million-plus

Worldwide Abortions – 1.5 billion-plus

Worldwide, abortions will be 3.2 million after 22 days in 2022. At this rate, they will be approaching 53 million by year-end

U.S. Abortions - 42 million babies from 1973 to 2019

U.S. Abortions – 893,000 in 2020

U.S. Abortions – 887,000 in 2019

U.S. Abortions – 872,000 in 2018

U.S. Abortions – 862,320 in 2017

Worldwide abortions - 365 million abortions from 2015 to 2019

Worldwide abortions are 73.3 million annually

Worldwide abortions 73.6 million annually from 2015 to 2019 (11)

U.S. Abortions in 2019 – 629,898

U.S. Abortions in 2018 – 619,591

Worldwide Abortions – 73 million per year

Websites

http://www.lifematt erstv.org/

http://www.numberofabortions.com/

https://www.worldometers.info/abortions/

https://www.statista.com/statistics/185274/number-of-legal-abortions-in-the-us-since-2000/

https://abort73.com/abortion_facts/us_abortion_statistics/

https://www.guttmacher.org/fact-sheet/induced-abortion-united-states

https://www.guttmacher.org/fact-sheet/induced-abortion-worldwide

https://pubmed.ncbi.nlm.nih.gov/32710833/

https://data.guttmacher.org/regions/table?region=37+38+39+40+41+44+45+47+46+105+106&topics=3&dataset=data

https://www.cdc.gov/mmwr/volumes/70/ss/ss7009a1.htm/

https://www.who.int/news-room/fact-sheets/detail/abortion

PRO-LIFE ABORTION NUMBERS

Life Matters TV Program

http://www.lifematt erstv.org/

Number of Abortions – Abortion Counter

http://www.numberofabortions.com/

U.S. ABORTIONS

60 MILLION-PLUS

60 million-plus - abortions since Roe vs. Wade in the United States (2018) - 60, 933,000 (1)

18 million-plus - Black babies aborted since Roe vs. Wade in the United States (2018) - 18,280,000 (2)

WORLDWIDE ABORTIONS

1.5 BILLION-PLUS

1.5 billion-plus - Babies aborted in the world since 1980 (2018) (3)

37 million-plus - Babies aborted in the world in 2018 (4)

Worldometer

Worldometer is a small, independent digital publisher wanting to present statistics to the world.

"Abortions worldwide this year"

https://www.worldometers.info/abortions/

Worldwide, abortions will be 3.2 million after 22 days in 2022. At this rate, they will be approaching 53 million by year-end

"3,228,000 on 1/28/22 at 2:30 EST, and it is changing every second." (5)

Statista

Number of legal abortions reported in the U.S. from 1973 to 2019

https://www.statista.com/statistics/185274/number-of-legal-abortions-in-the-us-since-2000/

U.S. ABORTIONS

42 MILLION BABIES
FROM 1973 TO 2019

An approximate number of 42 million babies were aborted from 1973 to 2019. (6)

Abort73.com

"US Abortion Statistics"

https://abort73.com/abortion_facts/us_abortion_statistics/

U.S. ABORTIONS

893,000 IN 2020

887,000 in 2019

872,000 in 2018

"Based on available state-level data, approximately 893,000 abortions took place in the United States in 2020. That's up from approximately 887,000 abortions in 2019 and 872,000 abortions in 2018." (7)

Sources

"Abort73.com," US Abortion Statistics, https://abort73.com/abortion_facts/us_abortion_statistics/, 1/28/22.

"Number of Abortions – Abortion Counter,"
Number of Abortions – Abortion Counter, http://www.numberofabortions.com/, 1/28/22.

"Statista," Number of legal abortions reported in the United States from 1973 to 2019, https://www.statista.com/statistics/185274/number-of-legal-abortions-in-the-us-since-2000/, 1/28/22

"Worldometer," Abortions worldwide this year, https://www.worldometers.info/abortions/, 1/28/22

PRO-CHOICE ABORTION NUMBERS

Guttmacher institute

Guttmacher Institute is an abortion rights research and policy organization.

"Induced Abortions in the United States"

https://www.guttmacher.org/fact-sheet/
induced-abortion-united-states

U.S. ABORTIONS

862,320 IN 2017

"Approximately 862,320 abortions were performed in 2017" (8)

Guttmacher Institute

Guttmacher Institute is an abortion rights research and policy organization.

"Unintended Pregnancy and Abortion Worldwide"

https://www.guttmacher.org/fact-sheet/
induced-abortion-worldwide

WORLDWIDE ABORTIONS

365 MILLION ABORTIONS
FROM 2015 TO 2019

"73 million abortions per year" for each year 2015, 2016, 2017, 2018, and 2019 for a total of 365 million abortions globally. **(9)**

National Library of Medicine

Lancet Global Health

Lancet Global Health is a global medical health journal.

https://pubmed.ncbi.nlm.nih.gov/32710833/

WORLDWIDE ABORTIONS ARE 73.3 MILLION ANNUALLY

"(totalling 73·3 million abortions annually [66·7-82·0]), corresponding to a global abortion rate of 39 abortions (36-44) per 1000 women aged 15-49 years." (10)

Guttmacher Institute

Guttmacher Institute is an abortion rights research and policy organization.

"Data Center"

https://data.guttmacher.org/regions/table?
region=37+38+39+40+41+44+45+47+46+105+106&topics=3&d
ataset=data

Worldwide abortions 73.6 million annually
from 2015 to 2019 (11)

Sources

"Guttmacher Institute," Data Center, https://data.guttmacher.org/
regions/table?
region=37+38+39+40+41+44+45+47+46+105+106&topics=3&d
ataset=data, 1/28/2022

"Guttmacher Institute," Induced Abortions in the
United States, https://www.guttmacher.org/fact-
sheet/induced-abortion-united-states,1/28/22.

"Guttmacher Institute," Unintended Pregnancy and
Abortion Worldwide, https://www.guttmacher.org/
fact-sheet/induced-abortion-worldwide, 1/28/22 .

"National Library of Medicine" Lancet Global Health: Unintended
pregnancy and abortion by income, region, and the legal status of

abortion: estimates from a comprehensive model for 1990-2019, https://pubmed.ncbi.nlm.nih.gov/32710833/, 1/28/22.

POLITICAL AGENCIES ABORTION NUMBERS

Centers for Disease Control and Prevention

"Morbidity and Mortality Weekly Report (MMWR)"

"Abortion Surveillance – United States, 2019"

https://www.cdc.gov/mmwr/volumes/70/ss/ss7009a1.htm/

U.S. ABORTIONS IN 2019

629,898

"Results: A total of 629,898 abortions for 2019 were reported to CDC from 49 reporting areas. Among 48 reporting areas with data each year during 2010–2019, in 2019, a total of 625,346 abortions were reported, the abortion rate was 11.4 abortions per 1,000 women aged 15–44 years, and the abortion ratio was 195 abortions per 1,000 live births. From 2018 to 2019, the total number of abortions increased 2% (from 614,820 total abortions), the abortion rate increased 0.9% (from 11.3 abortions per 1,000 women aged 15–44 years), and the abortion ratio increased 3% (from 189 abortions per 1,000 live births)." (12)

Centers for Disease Control and Prevention

"Morbidity and Mortality Weekly Report (MMWR)"

"Abortion Surveillance – United States, 2018"

https://www.cdc.gov/mmwr/volumes/69/ss/ss6907a1.htm/

U.S. ABORTIONS IN 2018

619,591

"A total of 619,591 abortions for 2018 were reported to CDC from 49 reporting areas." (13)

Centers for Disease Control and Prevention

"Morbidity and Mortality Weekly Report (MMWR)"

"Abortion Surveillance Reports for the United States"

You can access all the abortion surveillance reports from 1980 to 2019 on this website. (14)

https://www.cdc.gov/reproductivehealth/data_stats/index.htm

World Health Organization

"Abortion"

https://www.who.int/news-room/fact-sheets/detail/abortion

WORLDWIDE ABORTIONS

73 MILLION PER YEAR

"Around 73 million induced abortions take place worldwide each year" (15)

Sources

"Centers for Disease Control and Prevention," Abortion Surveillance – United States, 2019, https://www.cdc.gov/mmwr/volumes/70/ss/ss7009a1.htm, 1/28/22.

"Centers for Disease Control and Prevention," Abortion Surveillance – United States, 2018, "Centers for Disease Control and Prevention," Abortion Surveillance – United States, 2019, https://www.cdc.gov/mmwr/volumes/69/ss/ss6907a1.htm/, 1/28/22.

https://www.cdc.gov/reproductivehealth/data_stats/index.htm

"World Health Organization," Abortion, https://www.who.int/news-room/fact-sheets/detail/abortion, 1/28/22

OTHER DEATHS IN COMPARISON TO ABORTION

Total abortions to date 1,500,000,000 (16)

Estimate abortions per year 73,000,000

Total deaths 2019 worldwide 54,000,000 (17)

Communism related deaths 110,000,000 (18)

World War II deaths 60,000,000 (19)

Black Plague deaths 20,000,000 (20)

Hunger and hunger-related deaths – 9,000,000 per year (21)

Heart Disease deaths 8,900,000 per year (22)

Stroke deaths 6,100,00 per year (23)

Global covid deaths 5,662,713 (24)

Pulmonary disease death 3,300,00 per year (25)

Respiratory infection deaths 2,600,000 per year (26)

Homicide deaths 400,000 per year (27)

Natural disaster deaths 60,000 per year (28)

Terrorism related deaths – 21,000 per year (29)

Sources

"hawaii.edu," How Many Did Communist Regimes Murder?, https://hawaii.edu/powerkills/COM.ART.HTM, 1/28/22

"History," Black Death, https://www.history.com/topics/middle-ages/black-death, 1/28/22

"The National World War II Museum," Research Starters: Worldwide Deaths in World War II, https://www.nationalww2museum.org/students-teachers/student-resources/research-starters/research-starters-worldwide-deaths-world-war, 1/28/22

"Our World in Data," Homicides, https://ourworldindata.org/homicides, 1/28/22

"Our World in Data," Natural Disasters, https://ourworldindata.org/natural-disasters, 1/28/22

"Our World in Data," Terrorism, https://ourworldindata.org/terrorism, 1/28/22

"The World Counts," People Who Died From Hunger, https://www.theworldcounts.com/challenges/people-and-poverty/hunger-and-obesity/how-many-people-die-from-hunger-each-year/story, 1/28/22

"World Health Organization," The Top Ten Causes of Death, https://www.who.int/news-room/fact-sheets/detail/the-top-10-causes-of-death, 1/28/22

"Worldometer," Coronvirus Death Toll, https://www.worldometers.info/coronavirus/coronavirus-death-toll/, 1/28/22

ABOUT THE AUTHOR

Conrad Birmingham

Conrad Birmingham is a businessman who is retired, and he is trying to stay busy. He has no natural talent at writing any type of writing except Quality Assurance Programs, Business Plans, Bible Study Notes, Business Price Quotes, Business Memos, Loan Requests, Consulting Reports, and all things business. 

He has written poems for the past fifteen years. He has written three books of poetry, and he hopes you will enjoy reading them.

Conrad likes four stanzas with rhyming verses. They are called Quatrains, but he does not care. They are poems with four lines that rhyme. Also, he does not like punctuation. He does not use punctuation, allowing the verses to flow as they flow. He wants the reader to figure it out, and there are no participation trophies here.

This book is dear to his heart. He believes abortion is an atrocity. It is much worse than war, disease, or starvation. Conrad is writing a series of novels about abortion to bring awareness to the number of babies murdered through abortions. This is a serious subject, and to know the facts or the accurate numbers is essential. His book, "Abortion Facts," highlights these facts from the Pro-Life, Pro-Choice, and Political Organizations statistics.

He hopes you enjoy his writings, and he wishes you to visit his website, conradwriter.com, and Facebook page, https://www.facebook.com/profile.php?id=100071070078910. He would like for you to leave comments and reviews. He encourages you to ask him questions about his writings. Good or bad, he does not mind. He wants to get better at writing, and he believes the best way is to be criticized and pushed to be better.